HOW TO D

GEX ™

& the Gang

Written by Michael Teitelbaum
Illustrated by Ron Zalme

Troll

Special thanks to Brian Silva and the Crystal Dynamics GEX team,
and to Rand Marlis and Ruth Adams.

A Creative Media Applications Production
Art Direction by Fabia Wargin Design

GEX, the GEX character, and the related characters are trademarks of Crystal Dynamics. ©1999 Crystal Dynamics. Crystal Dynamics is a wholly owned subsidiary of Eidos Interactive, Inc. Eidos Interactive is a registered trademark of EIDOS, PLC. ®1999 Eidos. All rights reserved.

Published by Troll Communications L.L.C.

Printed in the United States of America.
ISBN 0-8167-6342-9
10 9 8 7 6 5 4 3 2 1

Introduction

GEX here. Deep Cover GEX, to you.

I've stopped doing my favorite thing in the entire world—watching TV—long enough to welcome you to this dynamite book. If you've followed my adventures as a secret agent, pirate, robot, mobster, army guy, kung fu star, and—well, the list of my talents goes on and on—then you're gonna love this book, baby!

You'll learn how to draw me and many of my enemies—both head shots and tail-slamming action pictures. You'll draw me as **Private GEX as I battle The Sarge** (*"Lock and load up—on plenty of paper, little lizard!"*), **Long John GEX as I square off against Skeleton Pirate** (*"Arrgh, me mateys, be sure to sharpen ye pencils!"*), **GEX Capone against Lenny Mobster** (*"This is a rubout—use your eraser if you make a mistake!"*), **and RoboGEX as I face a final confrontation with my ultimate enemy, that mechanical psycho, Rez** (*"You'll transform—into a great artist!"*).

Now, don't worry if your drawings aren't perfect the first time—it's déjà-draw all over again. In other words, keep practicing! In less time than it takes to shout "It's tail time!" you'll be drawing facial expressions, putting characters into action, and making up your own adventures in the Media Dimension.

My favorite kung fu movie—*The Nine Nasty Ninjas vs. General Chang's Radioactive Chickens*—is about to start. But before I go hunker down with my beloved remote control and a big bowl full of crunchy flies, here are a few things to keep in mind as you make your way through this awesome book:

1. **Draw lightly as you sketch.** You'll have plenty of time to darken your lines as you finish your drawing and fill in the details.

2. **Stay loose!** Let your hand and arm move freely. Don't grip your pencil like you're trying to crush Rez! Drawing should be relaxing and fun.

3. **Don't worry about mistakes—** that's why erasers were invented!

4. **Practice, and be patient.** It takes time to get good at drawing. So grab your pencil and get started. I'm outta here, baby!

Basic Shapes

circle

square

triangle

rectangle

oval

Everything you draw with your pencil is a two-dimensional flat shape, like the five basic shapes at the top of this page. However, using techniques you'll learn in this book, you can create the illusion of an actual three-dimensional object in your drawings. Look at the circle shown above. It is round and two-dimensional. Now pick up a ball. The ball is also round, but it is three-dimensional–an actual object. The trick to drawing believable characters is to create the illusion on paper that what you are drawing is three-dimensional (like the ball), even though it is really only two-dimensional (like the circle). Look at the drawing of the sphere below. The sphere is the three-dimensional "partner" to the circle. You can see that just by adding the two crisscrossing dotted lines to the drawing of the circle, you can create the illusion of the three-dimensional sphere. The same can be done with each of the shapes shown on this page. Practice drawing the two-dimensional shapes, then work on the 3-D shapes like the cube, pyramid, etc. After you've practiced for a while, you'll be ready to start drawing GEX!

sphere

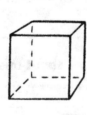
cube

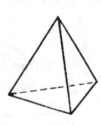
pyramid

cylinder

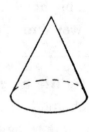
cone

GEX's Head

Because he's a gecko (and proud of it!), GEX's head is long, not round. So let's begin by drawing an oval shape. Then draw two lines, one vertical and one horizontal, to form a plus sign. In drawing, these two lines are called "crosshairs." They help you figure out where to place the facial features (eyes, nose, etc.). Next, draw a smaller oval and a semicircle (half-circle) at the top of the head oval. These will form GEX's eye.

1

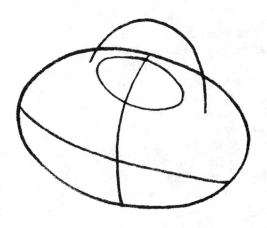

2

Now you can add more details to the eye. Draw a bean shape around the eye oval, and outline the pupil at the center. Shape the lower eyelid and the corners of the eye, as shown. Then draw a second semicircle at the top of the head to form GEX's other eye. Add the snout (also known as his nose) and his sly grin, as shown.

Next, draw GEX's chin and neck. Use a long curved line to create the chin. The neck is formed by another long curved line and three shorter lines. Draw the small curve that completes his second eye, and add details to his first eye, snout, and mouth, as shown.

3

4

Finally, blacken the pupil, leaving only a small white highlight, as shown. Notice the thickened line at the corner of GEX's mouth that brings to life his oh-so-confident gecko grin. Erase any extra lines, and your first drawing of GEX is complete!

Deep Cover Gecko

Now let's draw the entire GEX character. As with most character drawings, we begin with the head. Draw a large oval with intersecting crosshairs. Add a smaller oval and a semicircle on top (like you practiced on page 5). Then make the body shapes, as shown, for GEX's neck, body, and legs. It may take a little extra practice to get the shapes just right.

1

Next, draw a bean shape around the eye and outline the pupil, just like you did on page 5. Draw GEX's snout and mouth, and add a V shape to his neck. Follow the lines shown here to outline his arms, then draw two rectangles for his hands and a small circle for his thumb. Two curved lines on the body form his jacket, and three sweeping curves make up GEX's powerful tail. Shape his right leg, as shown, and complete this step by drawing his feet.

2

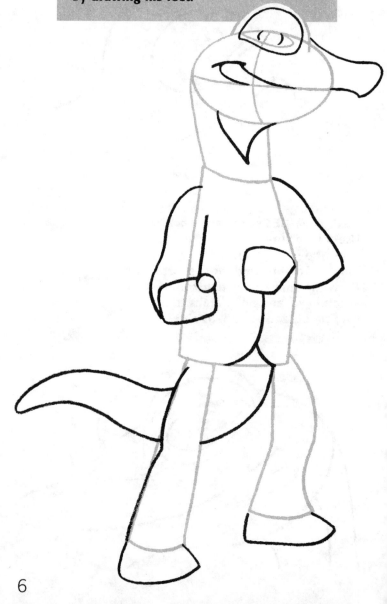

Draw GEX's second eye and his chin, and a curved line around the top of his head, as shown. Add lines to his mouth, neck, leg, and tail, as well. Now it's time to draw the finer details, like his fingers and toes. Copy them as you see them here. Don't forget his left kneecap! Follow the rectangular shapes and curves shown to make his collar and cravat, then add his fancy ruffled cuffs.

3

Finish your drawing by adding four short fold lines in GEX's cravat and some creases at his elbows. Two small circles make his buttons. Fill in his pupil, leaving a white highlight, erase any extra lines, and you're done. This is one sharp-dressing gecko!

4

Kung Fu GEX

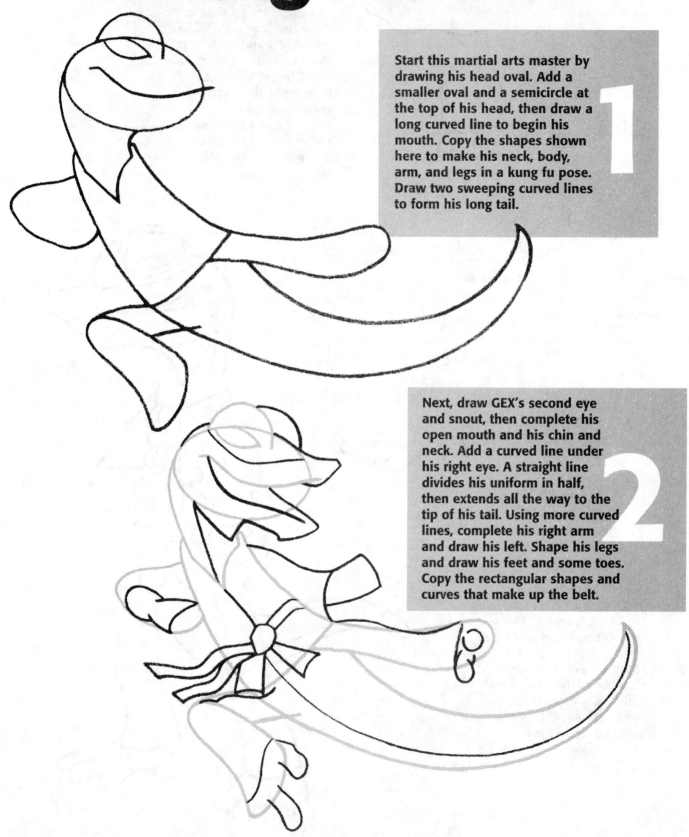

Start this martial arts master by drawing his head oval. Add a smaller oval and a semicircle at the top of his head, then draw a long curved line to begin his mouth. Copy the shapes shown here to make his neck, body, arm, and legs in a kung fu pose. Draw two sweeping curved lines to form his long tail.

1

Next, draw GEX's second eye and snout, then complete his open mouth and his chin and neck. Add a curved line under his right eye. A straight line divides his uniform in half, then extends all the way to the tip of his tail. Using more curved lines, complete his right arm and draw his left. Shape his legs and draw his feet and some toes. Copy the rectangular shapes and curves that make up the belt.

2

Draw his pupil and outline his eye and tongue. Draw the fingers on each hand as you see them here, and add a few more toes. There are many small fold lines in GEX's uniform, so look carefully to be sure you get them all.

3

To finish your drawing, just blacken the pupil, leaving a white highlight, and erase any extra lines. You've got Kung Fu GEX in action!

4

Private GEX

Start drawing this soldier with the usual head oval, but this time add a much larger semicircle on top (this will become his helmet) and a triangular shape to begin his eye. Draw the rest of the body shapes exactly as shown (notice that the arm is a V and the legs are two rectangles). These shapes will provide the framework for the rest of the figure.

1

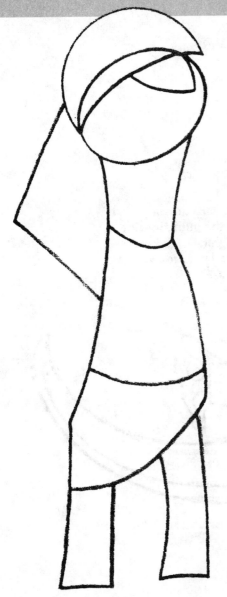

Now you are ready to add some details. Draw the eye and snout, then carefully follow the shapes shown to make his arms and hands, his collar, backpack, belt, and boots. And, of course, don't forget his all-powerful tail!

2

Complete the face in this step, by drawing GEX's second eye, pupil, and chin. Add fingers to his left hand and give the tail a dimension line. Now move on to the details of the helmet and uniform, such as the chin straps and pockets and the rest of his backpack. There are a lot of wrinkles and folds in Private GEX's uniform, so follow the example closely and keep practicing to make sure you don't miss anything!

3

Finally, blacken the pupil (leaving a white highlight) and add crisscross webbing to the helmet. Compare your drawing to this one to make sure you've put in all the details! When your picture is complete, erase any extra lines. Private GEX reporting for duty!

4

The Sarge

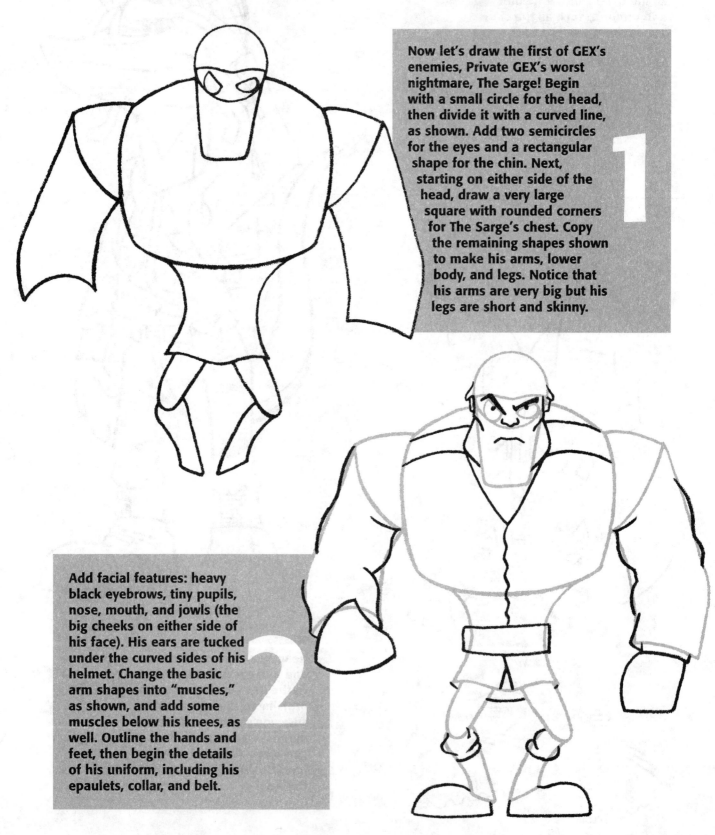

Now let's draw the first of GEX's enemies, Private GEX's worst nightmare, The Sarge! Begin with a small circle for the head, then divide it with a curved line, as shown. Add two semicircles for the eyes and a rectangular shape for the chin. Next, starting on either side of the head, draw a very large square with rounded corners for The Sarge's chest. Copy the remaining shapes shown to make his arms, lower body, and legs. Notice that his arms are very big but his legs are short and skinny.

1

Add facial features: heavy black eyebrows, tiny pupils, nose, mouth, and jowls (the big cheeks on either side of his face). His ears are tucked under the curved sides of his helmet. Change the basic arm shapes into "muscles," as shown, and add some muscles below his knees, as well. Outline the hands and feet, then begin the details of his uniform, including his epaulets, collar, and belt.

2

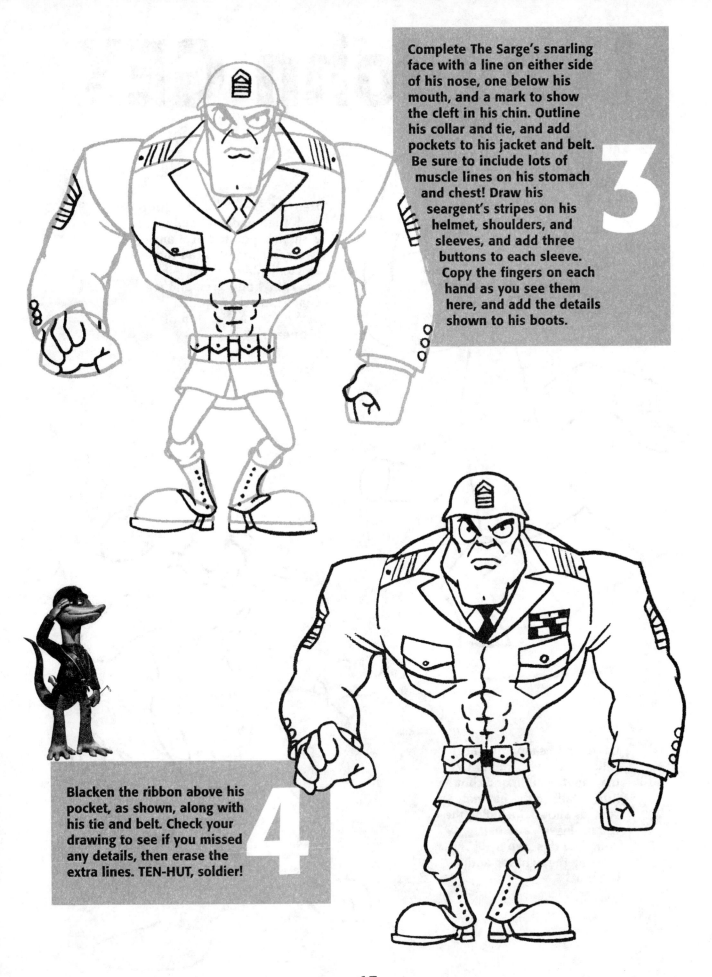

Complete The Sarge's snarling face with a line on either side of his nose, one below his mouth, and a mark to show the cleft in his chin. Outline his collar and tie, and add pockets to his jacket and belt. Be sure to include lots of muscle lines on his stomach and chest! Draw his seargent's stripes on his helmet, shoulders, and sleeves, and add three buttons to each sleeve. Copy the fingers on each hand as you see them here, and add the details shown to his boots.

3

Blacken the ribbon above his pocket, as shown, along with his tie and belt. Check your drawing to see if you missed any details, then erase the extra lines. TEN-HUT, soldier!

4

13

Long John GEX

Here's GEX as a pirate. Start with the head oval and add a smaller pointed oval and two semicircles to the top, as you've been doing. Next, copy the body, arm, and leg shapes, as shown, then outline the hat on top of his head.

1

Continue to shape the face: Outline the eyes, and draw the snout, mouth, and chin. Add details to the hat and coat, as shown, including the collar, sleeves, and belt. Complete this step by drawing the right leg and left foot.

2

3 Complete the face with the details shown, including the pupil and tongue. Draw the skull and crossbones, and add stripes to the hat and coat and a buckle to the belt. Now you can give Long John GEX his sword, hook, and pegleg! Copy them as you see them here. Add toes to GEX's foot—and be sure to include that tail!

4 Use this final pose to make sure you haven't missed any details. Fill in the eye, leaving a white highlight, and erase any extra lines. ARRRGGH, matey!

Skeleton Pirate

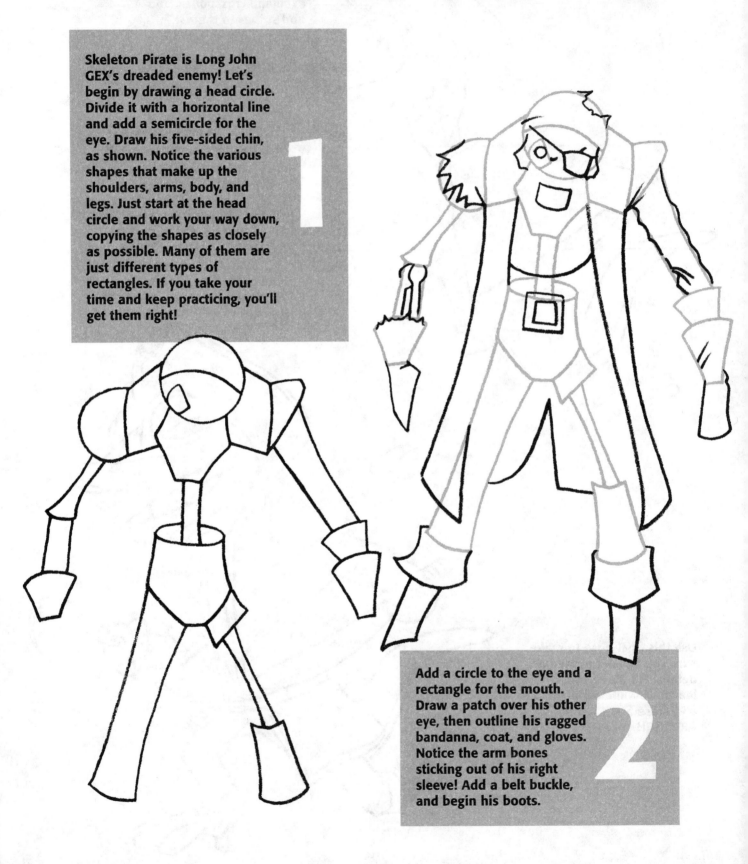

1 Skeleton Pirate is Long John GEX's dreaded enemy! Let's begin by drawing a head circle. Divide it with a horizontal line and add a semicircle for the eye. Draw his five-sided chin, as shown. Notice the various shapes that make up the shoulders, arms, body, and legs. Just start at the head circle and work your way down, copying the shapes as closely as possible. Many of them are just different types of rectangles. If you take your time and keep practicing, you'll get them right!

2 Add a circle to the eye and a rectangle for the mouth. Draw a patch over his other eye, then outline his ragged bandanna, coat, and gloves. Notice the arm bones sticking out of his right sleeve! Add a belt buckle, and begin his boots.

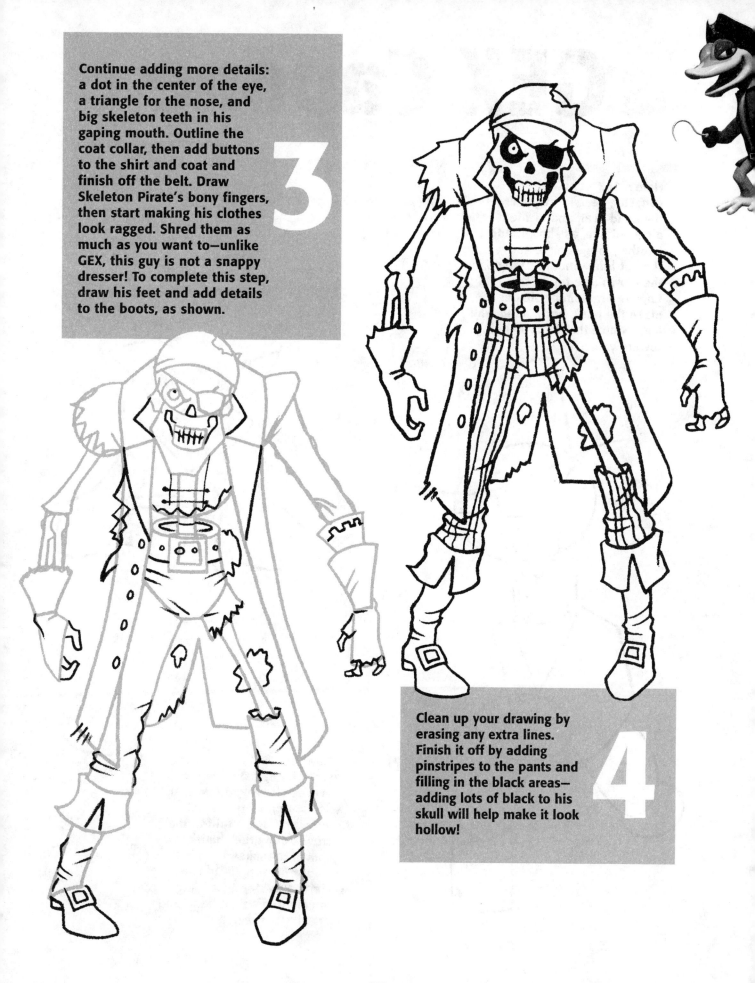

Continue adding more details: a dot in the center of the eye, a triangle for the nose, and big skeleton teeth in his gaping mouth. Outline the coat collar, then add buttons to the shirt and coat and finish off the belt. Draw Skeleton Pirate's bony fingers, then start making his clothes look ragged. Shred them as much as you want to—unlike GEX, this guy is not a snappy dresser! To complete this step, draw his feet and add details to the boots, as shown.

3

Clean up your drawing by erasing any extra lines. Finish it off by adding pinstripes to the pants and filling in the black areas—adding lots of black to his skull will help make it look hollow!

4

GEX Capone

Here's GEX as an old-time gangster, see? To begin, draw the head oval, and divide it with a curved line, as shown. Add another, longer curve above it for the hat brim, and a rectangle for the crown (the top of the hat). Copy the remaining shapes to make the neck, body, hand, and legs. Notice that he is stepping toward you.

1

Now let's add detail to the face and hat. Outline the eye, as shown, and draw the snout. Complete the hat brim, and add a fold to the crown. Copy the shapes shown to make his coat. Notice his turned-up collar. Finish this step by adding fingers to his right hand and drawing his feet.

2

18

It's tail time! Draw GEX's long, curving tail, along with his pupil and chin and the fingers on his left hand. Then continue to add details to the face and clothes, as shown.

3

Blacken the tie and pupil (leaving a white highlight). Compare your drawing to this final pose to check for details you might have missed, and erase any extra lines. If you like, color GEX Capone in with dark colors. Now he's ready to go up against his enemy, Lenny Mobster!

4

Lenny Mobster

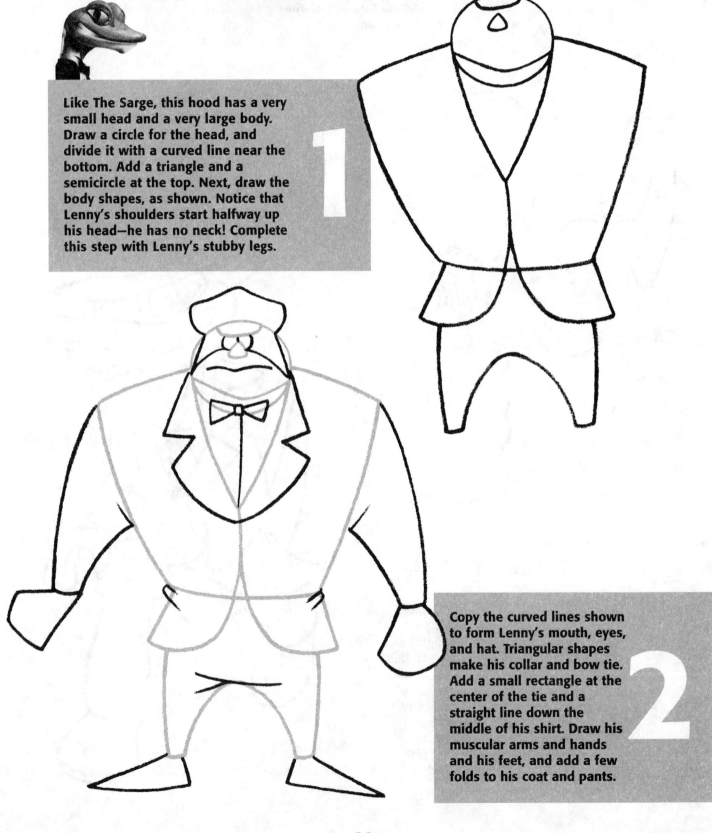

1 Like The Sarge, this hood has a very small head and a very large body. Draw a circle for the head, and divide it with a curved line near the bottom. Add a triangle and a semicircle at the top. Next, draw the body shapes, as shown. Notice that Lenny's shoulders start halfway up his head—he has no neck! Complete this step with Lenny's stubby legs.

2 Copy the curved lines shown to form Lenny's mouth, eyes, and hat. Triangular shapes make his collar and bow tie. Add a small rectangle at the center of the tie and a straight line down the middle of his shirt. Draw his muscular arms and hands and his feet, and add a few folds to his coat and pants.

Finish off the face by adding pupils (and some wrinkles around his eyes), ears, and a bulging lower lip. Be sure to include Lenny's crooked tooth! Complete his collar, and add buttons to his shirt and coat. Draw fingers on each hand, as shown, and add details to his shoes.

3

A crisscrossing striped pattern on Lenny's suit and hat will give him the "cheap hoodlum" look he needs. Double-check the details, clean up your drawing by erasing any extra lines, and Lenny's ready to battle GEX Capone!

4

Gladiator GEX

Let's send GEX back in time by drawing him as a Roman gladiator. Begin with an oval for the head. Draw a curved horizontal line extending beyond the oval to begin the mouth, then add a smaller oval and a semicircle at the top for the eye. Copy the shape shown to start his helmet, then draw the neck, body, arms, and leg as you see them here. Complete this step by adding two sweeping lines for his tail.

1

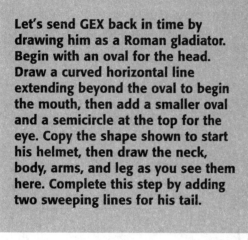

Starting at the top, add two more curved shapes to the helmet, then draw the snout and outline the eye with a larger oval. Add details to the neck and body, as shown, including the hands, the right leg, and three toes on the left foot. Notice the armor on his shoulders and knees.

2

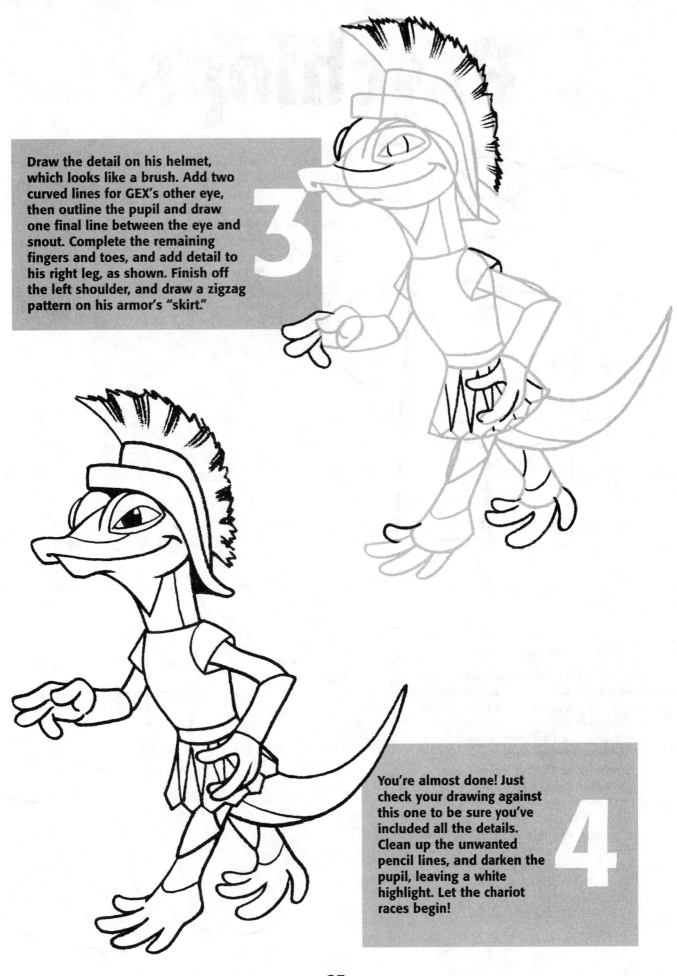

3 Draw the detail on his helmet, which looks like a brush. Add two curved lines for GEX's other eye, then outline the pupil and draw one final line between the eye and snout. Complete the remaining fingers and toes, and add detail to his right leg, as shown. Finish off the left shoulder, and draw a zigzag pattern on his armor's "skirt."

4 You're almost done! Just check your drawing against this one to be sure you've included all the details. Clean up the unwanted pencil lines, and darken the pupil, leaving a white highlight. Let the chariot races begin!

Psychlops

To draw this one-eyed enemy of Gladiator GEX, start with a square for Psychlops' head but curve the top of the square. Overlap two circles in the middle of the square for his eye and nose. Two sweeping lines extending out from the upper circle through the top of his head begin his horns. Make the rest of the body out of rectangles and circles, as you see here.

1

Start adding details to the face: Draw a smaller circle inside the top circle you made in step 1, then complete his nose and mouth, as shown. Use two more curved lines to finish off each horn, and add some fur to the top of his head. Now draw his left arm and hand and add fingers and a wristband to his right. Outline Psychlops' club as you see it here, then draw his lower legs and hooves. Finally, add his tunic, which drapes over his left shoulder, and a belt with a square buckle.

2

24

Complete the details on the face and head. Draw a half circle for the pupil and a wrinkle on either side of the eye, then add two big teeth and the lower lip. Put stripes on each horn and three triangular spikes on the head of the club, as well as some details on the handle. Add two more fingers and two nails to the right hand, and outline the knuckles on the left. Draw a wristband on his left arm, then add lots of furry edges to his tunic and ankles. To finish this step, draw four muscle lines on his chest and divide each hoof with two lines.

3

Just add spots to the tunic and blacken his pupil (leaving a white highlight) and the gap between his teeth. Check to be sure you've include all the details, and don't forget to erase your extra lines. Psychlops is one scary looking beast!

4

25

RoboGEX

Blast into the super high-tech world of the future with RoboGEX! This figure is pretty complicated, so just take it a step at a time and keep practicing. Begin with the head oval. Draw a curved horizontal line extending beyond the oval to begin the mouth, then add a smaller oval at the top for the eye. Notice the "crest" shape on his head. This will become his helmet. Draw two straight lines for his neck, then carefully copy the remaining shapes shown to form the body, arms, and legs.

1

Now let's fill in some of the details. Outline the right eye and add a curved line for the left, then draw the snout and mouth. Add two lines to the helmet and a square shape to the side of his head, then start to copy the angular shapes shown to make the mechanical details on the body, arms, and legs. Be sure to include his left hand and his feet. As always, two sweeping curves form GEX's tail.

2

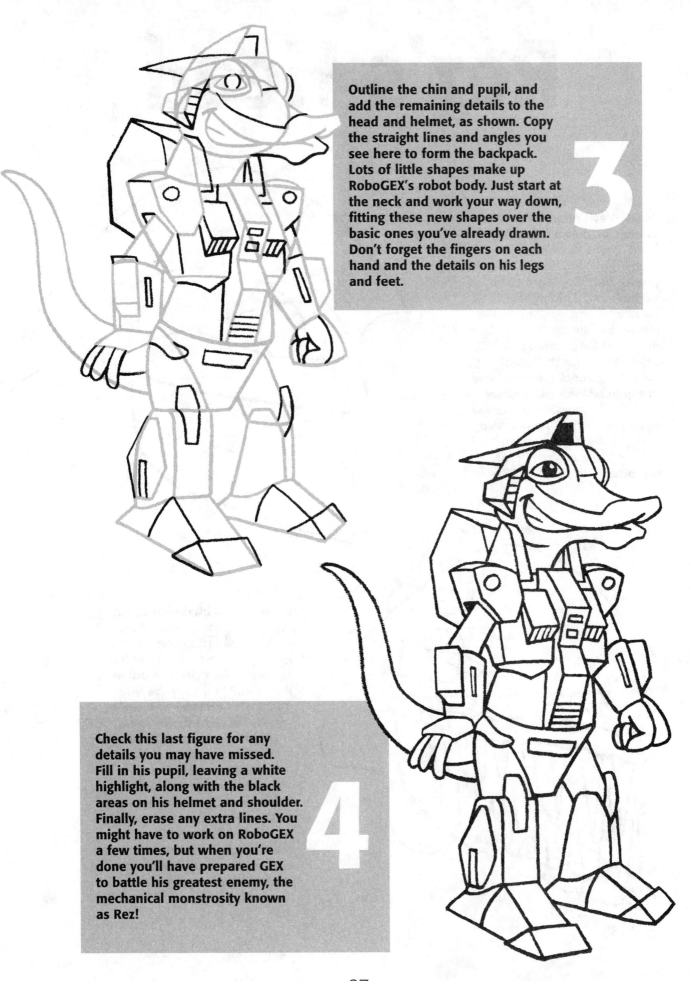

Outline the chin and pupil, and add the remaining details to the head and helmet, as shown. Copy the straight lines and angles you see here to form the backpack. Lots of little shapes make up RoboGEX's robot body. Just start at the neck and work your way down, fitting these new shapes over the basic ones you've already drawn. Don't forget the fingers on each hand and the details on his legs and feet.

3

Check this last figure for any details you may have missed. Fill in his pupil, leaving a white highlight, along with the black areas on his helmet and shoulder. Finally, erase any extra lines. You might have to work on RoboGEX a few times, but when you're done you'll have prepared GEX to battle his greatest enemy, the mechanical monstrosity known as Rez!

4

Rez's Head

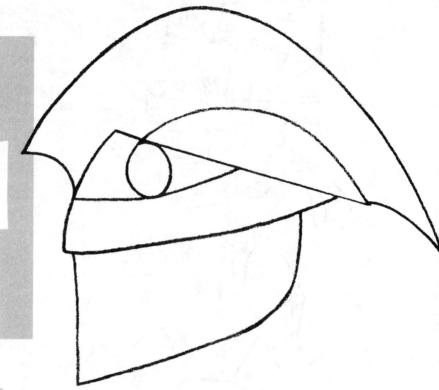

Rez, the evil ruler of the Media Dimension, has a fierce, metallic head. Begin by drawing the large triangular shape in the center (notice that the edges curve slightly) and dividing it with a horizontal line. Add an oval above the line for the eye, then draw two long curves above the triangle to form the top of the helmet. Connect the upper line to the head with two shorter curved lines, as shown. Outline Rez's jaw with another sweeping curve at the bottom of your drawing, and connect it to the forehead with a straight line.

1

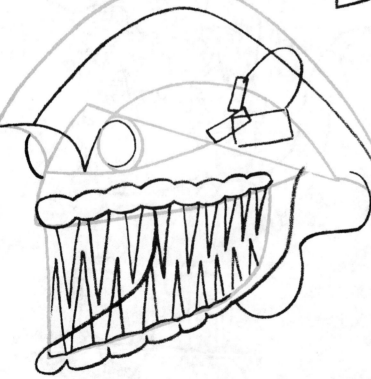

2

Divide the helmet with another long curve, then shape the front with two shorter curved lines. Add a second circle to the left eye and a half circle to outline the right. Then copy the three rectangles and the semicircle at the back of the helmet. Another sweeping curve divides the jaw in half, then forms Rez's bumpy lower lip. Copy the same bumpy look for the upper lip. There are lots of teeth to draw, but they're basically just triangles. Add one more wavy line, as shown, to connect the jaw and the helmet.

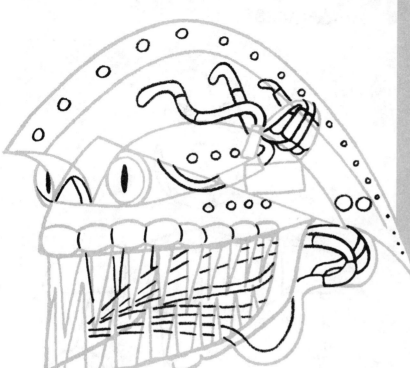

Blacken in Rez's long narrow pupils, and add some detail lines between his eyes. Lots of small circles make the rivets on his helmet. The wormlike shapes running through Rez's head are actually wires. They're bunched at the top of the helmet and also enter the mouth like a "tongue." Copy the general shapes you see here, but draw as many wires as you want—the more, the creepier! Finish this step by adding some short vertical lines to the upper lip and completing the chin.

3

Check this final drawing against yours for any missed details. Clean up the pencil lines and you're done! Don't worry if your drawing doesn't match this one exactly. As long as he's scary looking, you've captured Rez—on paper, that is!

4

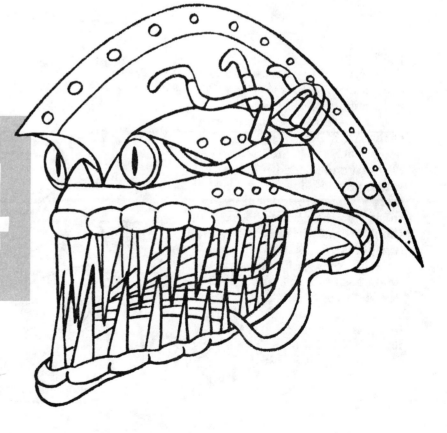

Rez

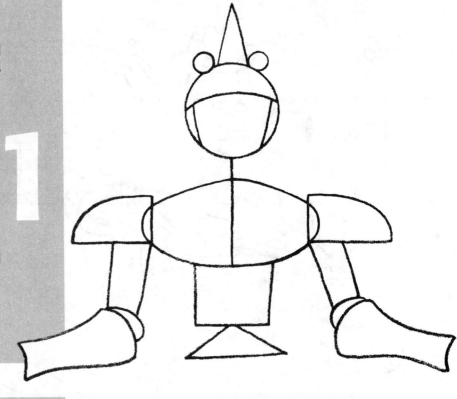

1 Now let's draw the full figure of this transistorized terror. Begin with a medium-sized circle for the head, and divide it with a horizontal curved line. Add two vertical lines in the lower part of the circle, as shown, then draw a triangle and two small circles on top. Notice that the head is a simpler shape in this front view than it is when it's drawn from the side (page 28). Draw in the oval shape for Rez's chest, and connect it to the head with a vertical line that divides the chest in half. Then add the shoulders and arms, as you see them here. Make sure they are symmetrical (the same size and shape on each side of the guideline running down the center of his chest). Add a rectangle and a triangle below the chest to form the rest of the body.

2 The curve you drew across the head circle becomes the top row of Rez's metal lips. Add the bottom row of lips along the bottom edge of the circle. Draw a short vertical line in each small circle to make his eyes, and divide his helmet with an upside-down Y and V. Four more V shapes form his neck and collar. Add the details shown to his shoulders and chest, including the first of his wormlike wires. Then draw his arms, including a pointed fin on each forearm, and his hands. To complete this step, draw three narrow rectangles and five triangles to make the jets that flame from the bottom of his body.

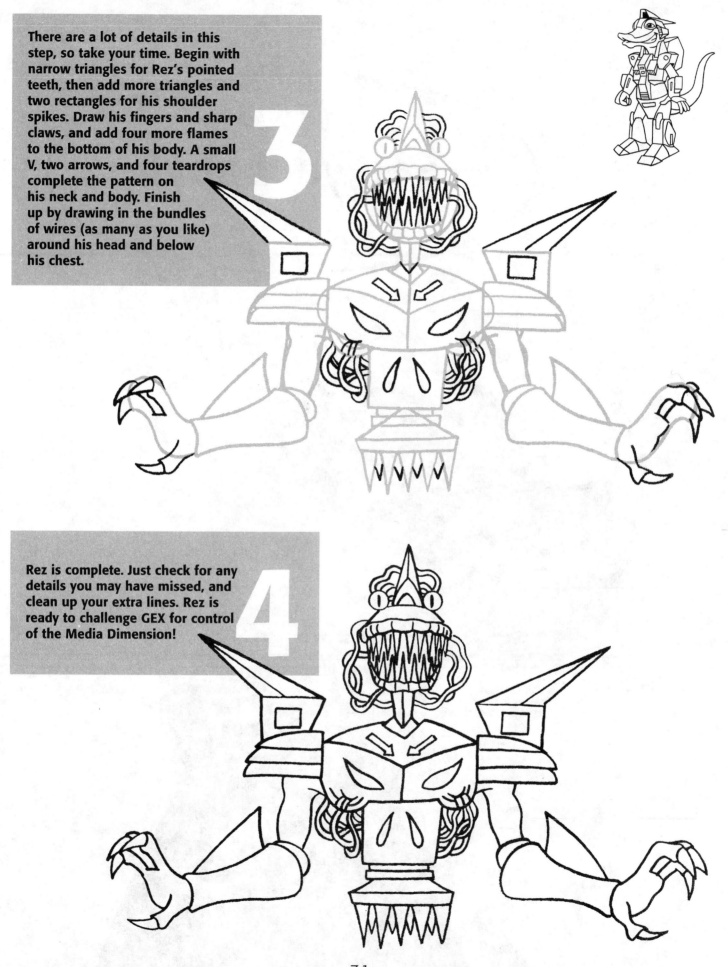

There are a lot of details in this step, so take your time. Begin with narrow triangles for Rez's pointed teeth, then add more triangles and two rectangles for his shoulder spikes. Draw his fingers and sharp claws, and add four more flames to the bottom of his body. A small V, two arrows, and four teardrops complete the pattern on his neck and body. Finish up by drawing in the bundles of wires (as many as you like) around his head and below his chest.

3

Rez is complete. Just check for any details you may have missed, and clean up your extra lines. Rez is ready to challenge GEX for control of the Media Dimension!

4

31